Pebble™ Plus

### Dinosaurs and Prehistoric Animals

# American Mastodon

by Carol K. Lindeen

**Consulting Editor:** Gail Saunders-Smith, PhD

Consultant: Jack Horner, Curator of Paleontology
Museum of the Rockies
Bozeman, Montana

Capstone press

Mankato, Minnesota

Pebble Plus is published by Capstone Press,
151 Good Counsel Drive, P.O. Box 669, Mankato, Minnesota 56002.
www.capstonepress.com

1 2 3 4 5 6 10 09 08 07 06 05

*Library of Congress Cataloging-in-Publication Data*
Lindeen, Carol K., 1976–
    American mastodon / by Carol K. Lindeen.
    p. cm.—(Pebble plus. Dinosaurs and prehistoric animals)
    Includes bibliographical references and index.
    ISBN-13: 978-0-7368-4255-6 (hardcover)
    ISBN-10: 0-7368-4255-1 (hardcover)
    ISBN-13: 978-0-7368-6128-1 (softcover pbk.)
    ISBN-10: 0-7368-6128-9 (softcover pbk.)
    1. Mastodon—North America—Juvenile literature. I. Title. II. Series.
QE882.U7L56 2006
569'.67—dc22                               2004026766

Summary: Simple text and illustrations present the life of American mastodon, how it looked, and its behavior.

**Editorial Credits**
Sarah L. Schuette, editor; Linda Clavel, set designer; Bobbi J. Dey, book designer; Wanda Winch, photo researcher

**Illustration and Photo Credits**
Jon Hughes, illustrator
Russell Gooday, 3D Content
Visuals Unlimited/Albert Copley, 21

## Note to Parents and Teachers

The Dinosaurs and Prehistoric Animals set supports national science standards related to the evolution of life. This book describes and illustrates American mastodon. The images support early readers in understanding the text. The repetition of words and phrases helps early readers learn new words. This book also introduces early readers to subject-specific vocabulary words, which are defined in the Glossary section. Early readers may need assistance to read some words and to use the Table of Contents, Glossary, Read More, Internet Sites, and Index sections of the book.

# Table of Contents

# Shaggy Mammals

American mastodons

were prehistoric mammals.

They had shaggy brown hair.

American mastodons
lived during the Ice Age.
They lived about 3.5 million
years ago in North America.

# How American Mastodons Looked

American mastodons
were about the size
of elephants.
They were about 8 feet
(2.4 meters) tall.

American mastodons
had thick legs.
They roamed near
lakes, swamps, and ponds.

American mastodons
had long trunks.
Their trunks sucked up water
and squirted it
into their mouths.

American mastodons
had two long tusks.
Their tusks were curved
and strong.

# What American Mastodons Did

American mastodons
grazed in herds.
They knocked down leaves
and twigs with their tusks.

American mastodons
ate branches from trees.
They crushed their food
with bumpy teeth.

# The End of American Mastodons

American mastodons died
about 10,000 years ago.
No one knows why
they all died. You can see
American mastodon fossils
in museums.

# Glossary

fossil—the remains or traces of an animal or
a plant, preserved as rock

graze—to eat plants that are growing in an area

herd—a large group of animals

Ice Age—a period of time when large sheets
of ice covered parts of the world

mammal—a warm-blooded animal with a
backbone; female mammals feed milk to
their young.

museum—a place where objects of art, history,
or science are shown

prehistoric—very, very old; prehistoric means
belonging to a time before history was
written down.

tusk—one of a pair of long, pointed teeth

# Read More

**Frost, Helen.** *Woolly Mammoth.* Pebble Plus: Dinosaurs and Prehistoric Animals. Mankato, Minn.: Capstone Press, 2005.

**Goecke, Michael P.** *American Mastodon.* Prehistoric Animals. Buddy Books. Edina, Minn.: Abdo, 2004.

**Goodman, Susan E.** *On This Spot: An Expedition Back Through Time.* New York: Greenwillow Books, 2004.

# Internet Sites

FactHound offers a safe, fun way to find Internet sites related to this book. All of the sites on FactHound have been researched by our staff.

Here's how:

1. Visit *www.facthound.com*

2. Type in this special code **0736842551** for age-appropriate sites. Or enter a search word related to this book for a more general search.

3. Click on the **Fetch It** button.

FactHound will fetch the best sites for you!

# Index

Word Count: 132
Grade: 1
Early-Intervention Level: 17